Printed by
Libri Plureos GmbH · Friedensallee 273
22763 Hamburg · Germany

Chat GPT: How It Works and How to Earn with the Use of Artificial Intelligence Technology

Expand Your Business and Gain a Competitive Edge with the Comprehensive Guide to Harnessing Chat GPT, the Cutting-Edge Artificial Intelligence Technology, to Create Customized Chatbots, Provide Personalized Responses, and Utilize Technology for Advertising, Generating Innovative Revenue, and Boosting Your Digital Presence.

Personal Evolution

Chat GPT (Generative Pre-trained Transformer) is an Artificial Intelligence technology developed by OpenAI, which utilizes advanced deep learning algorithms to generate coherent and relevant responses to user questions. The Chat GPT technology is based on the principle of "self-learning," meaning it can continuously learn from interactions with users, constantly improving its ability to generate increasingly accurate and pertinent responses.

The functioning of Chat GPT relies on an artificial neural network that is trained on an enormous corpus of natural language texts, sourced from reliable outlets such as Wikipedia, books, and newspaper articles. Thanks to this training, Chat GPT's neural network can understand the context of users' questions and generate coherent and relevant responses.

In addition to its capability to generate increasingly accurate and pertinent responses, the Chat GPT technology is capable of recognizing and responding to a wide range of questions and requests, both in natural language and technical jargon, making it extremely versatile and adaptable to various contexts.

The use of Chat GPT is spreading across different sectors, such as finance, healthcare, education, and marketing, revolutionizing the way businesses interact with their customers and consumers.

In summary, Chat GPT is a cutting-edge Artificial Intelligence technology capable of generating increasingly precise and pertinent responses to user questions. Thanks to its continuous learning ability and versatility, the Chat GPT technology is revolutionizing the way businesses interact with their customers and consumers, opening new business opportunities, and improving the user experience.

Many companies are leveraging the Chat GPT technology to enhance the user experience and create new business opportunities. Here are some examples of companies using Chat GPT:

Microsoft: Microsoft has integrated Chat GPT technology into its virtual assistance platform, Microsoft Virtual Agent, which provides support to customers on a wide range of technical and product-related issues.

Airbnb: Airbnb uses Chat GPT technology to offer personalized assistance to its users through the in-app messaging system. The Chat GPT technology helps hosts and guests respond to common questions and resolve issues more quickly.

Mastercard: Mastercard has developed a chatbot based on Chat GPT technology to assist customers in managing their finances, providing information on accounts, transactions, and available balances.

The New York Times: The New York Times has utilized Chat GPT technology to create a virtual assistant called "The News Quiz," which challenges users to answer questions about the news and provides personalized feedback based on their responses.

Hugging Face: Hugging Face is a company that specializes in developing customized chatbots for businesses using Chat GPT technology. Thanks to their expertise, Hugging Face has been able to create innovative and highly intelligent chatbots for companies of various sizes and industries.

These are just a few examples of companies that are using Chat GPT technology to enhance their service offerings and create new business opportunities. Due to its versatility and continuous learning capabilities, Chat GPT technology is becoming increasingly popular among companies worldwide.

The use of Chat GPT by businesses offers numerous advantages, including:

Improved User Experience: Chat GPT technology allows companies to provide their users with quick, accurate, and personalized responses to their questions and requests. This enhances the user experience, increases customer satisfaction, and improves the company's reputation.

Increased Efficiency: Thanks to Chat GPT's ability to automate many customer interactions, companies can reduce the time and resources required to provide assistance and support to their customers. This enables them to handle a higher volume of requests with fewer resources.

Cost Reduction: Automating customer interactions allows companies to reduce the costs associated with managing customer support services. This can lead to significant cost savings for businesses.

Enhanced Scalability: Chat GPT technology enables companies to handle a higher volume of customer interactions without the need to hire additional personnel. This allows businesses to scale their service offerings rapidly and efficiently.

Improved Data Quality: Thanks to Chat GPT's ability to gather and analyze large amounts of data, companies can gain valuable insights into their customers and their needs. This enables businesses to improve the quality of their data and make more informed decisions about their business strategy.

The Chat GPT technology uses data analysis to improve the quality of data collected during interactions with users. Specifically, Chat GPT employs natural language processing (NLP) and machine learning techniques to extract meaningful information from the collected data and improve its understanding of user needs and requirements.

Here's how data analysis works in Chat GPT to enhance data quality:

Data Collection: Chat GPT gathers data during interactions with users, such as questions posed by users and responses generated by the technology. These data are then processed and analyzed to extract useful information.

Data Preprocessing: Before analyzing the data, Chat GPT performs a data preprocessing operation, which involves a series of data cleaning and normalization techniques. These techniques help to remove any noise or ambiguity from the data and make it more coherent and consistent.

Data Analysis: After data preprocessing, Chat GPT utilizes natural language processing (NLP) and machine learning techniques to extract meaningful information from the collected data. For instance, the technology can analyze the data to identify common issues faced by users and areas for improvement in their service offerings.

Insight Generation: Based on the analyzed data, Chat GPT generates valuable insights to improve its service offerings. For example, the technology can suggest new features to add to its platform or enhancements to its customer support strategy.

Model Training: To continually improve the quality of the analyzed data, Chat GPT continuously trains its machine learning model on new data collected during interactions with users. This allows the technology to constantly enhance its ability to extract meaningful information from the data and generate useful insights to improve its service offerings.

Let's consider an e-commerce company that is using Chat GPT technology to provide customer assistance through its website. The company has noticed that many users utilizing the chatbot service complain about the difficulty of finding the products they are looking for on the website.

To improve data quality and better understand user needs, the company has used Chat GPT to analyze the data collected during user interactions with the chatbot. The technology has extracted meaningful information from the data, such as the most common search terms used by users and the products they are seeking.

Based on this information, the company has made some modifications to its website, such as enhancing site navigation and adding new features to help users find products more easily. Additionally, the company has improved the quality of product information on the website, including more detailed descriptions and high-quality images.

Thanks to the insights extracted by Chat GPT, the company gained a better understanding of user needs and made significant improvements to its service offerings. This has enhanced the user experience on the website and increased customer satisfaction.

In summary, the use of Chat GPT has enabled companies to better understand user needs and make significant improvements to their service offerings, enhancing the user experience on their websites and increasing customer satisfaction.

Here are some examples of companies that have utilized Chat GPT technology to improve their services:

Spotify: Spotify used Chat GPT technology to analyze data collected during user interactions with their music streaming service. This allowed them to better understand users' musical preferences and provide more accurate personalized playlists and artist recommendations.

American Express: American Express utilized Chat GPT technology to analyze data collected during customer interactions with their customer service. This helped them gain better insights into their customers' needs and offer personalized assistance and quicker responses to their queries.

Uber: Uber employed Chat GPT technology to analyze data collected during user interactions with their ride-sharing service. This enabled them to better understand user needs and enhance the accuracy of driver arrival time predictions.

Coca-Cola: Coca-Cola utilized Chat GPT technology to analyze data collected during user interactions with their website and social media activities. This allowed them to gain a better understanding of their consumers' preferences and create more effective and personalized marketing messages.

Mastercard: Mastercard used Chat GPT technology to analyze data collected during customer interactions with their customer service. This helped them gain insights into their customers' needs and offer more effective personalized assistance.

There are numerous resources available to help companies implement Chat GPT. Here are some suggestions on where to find further information:

OpenAI Documentation: OpenAI, the team that developed Chat GPT technology, provides comprehensive documentation on the technology's features and how to use it. The documentation is available on OpenAI's website and includes detailed guides and tutorials for implementing Chat GPT.

Developer Communities: There are numerous online developer communities discussing Chat GPT implementation and sharing ideas and tips.

For example, the OpenAI subreddit on Reddit is a valuable resource for finding information and resources on Chat GPT technology.

Online Courses: Many online courses are available to learn how to use Chat GPT technology. These courses can be helpful for understanding the basics of the technology and acquiring skills for implementation.

Specialized Companies: There are also companies specialized in Chat GPT implementation that can provide support and consultancy to businesses for implementing the technology. These companies can offer assistance in designing and developing customized solutions for specific business needs.

Implementation di Chat GPT requires a set of technical skills, including:

Programming Language Knowledge: To implement Chat GPT, a deep understanding of a programming language like Python is necessary, as the technology uses machine learning models and natural language processing algorithms.

Machine Learning Knowledge: Chat GPT relies on machine learning technology to process data and enhance its natural language analysis capabilities. Thus, a basic understanding of machine learning concepts such as regression, classification, clustering, and deep learning algorithms is required.

Natural Language Understanding: In order to implement Chat GPT, a thorough understanding of natural language and natural language processing techniques like semantic and syntactic analysis, text generation, and text classification is essential.

Experience with Natural Language Processing Tools: Familiarity with natural language processing tools such as Natural Language Toolkit (NLTK), Spacy, TensorFlow, and PyTorch is necessary.

Cloud Computing Knowledge: Chat GPT requires the use of cloud computing resources for data processing and model training. Hence, a basic understanding of cloud computing concepts and platforms like Amazon Web Services (AWS) or Microsoft Azure is necessary.

In summary, the implementation of Chat GPT demands a variety of technical skills, including proficiency in programming languages, machine learning, natural language processing, natural language processing tools, and cloud computing. However, there are also pre-packaged solutions available on the market that can assist businesses in implementing Chat GPT with fewer technical skills required.

Several pre-packaged solutions are available on the market for implementing Chat GPT without the need for advanced machine learning or natural language processing knowledge. Here are some of the most popular solutions:

Dialogflow: Dialogflow is a cloud-based natural language processing platform that allows the creation of advanced chatbots and voice assistants without requiring extensive machine learning or natural language processing expertise. Dialogflow utilizes Google's natural language processing algorithm to analyze user queries and provide appropriate responses.

IBM Watson Assistant: IBM Watson Assistant is a cloud-based chatbot platform that allows the creation of custom chatbots using natural language processing and machine learning. IBM Watson Assistant also includes advanced features such as context understanding and intent analysis to provide more accurate responses.

Botpress: Botpress is an open-source chatbot platform that enables the creation of custom chatbots using natural language processing and machine learning. Botpress also includes advanced features like intent analysis and text generation to provide more accurate responses.

Rasa: Rasa is an open-source chatbot platform that enables the creation of custom chatbots using natural language processing and machine learning. Rasa also includes advanced features such as intent analysis and text generation to provide more accurate responses.

TARS: TARS is a cloud-based chatbot platform that allows the creation of custom chatbots using a drag-and-drop visual interface. TARS also includes advanced features like intent analysis and text generation to provide more accurate responses.

In summary, there are several pre-packaged solutions available on the market to implement Chat GPT without requiring advanced machine learning or natural language processing knowledge. These solutions, such as Dialogflow, IBM Watson Assistant, Botpress, Rasa, and TARS, offer advanced capabilities to create custom chatbots and advanced virtual assistants.

Additionally, there are various pre-packaged solutions available to integrate Chat GPT with social media, allowing businesses to create custom chatbots and advanced virtual assistants that can interact with their customers on social media platforms. Some popular solutions include:

ManyChat: ManyChat is a cloud-based chatbot platform that allows the creation of custom chatbots for Facebook Messenger, Instagram, WhatsApp, and other messaging channels. ManyChat uses natural language processing to analyze user requests and provide appropriate responses.

Chatfuel: Chatfuel is a cloud-based chatbot platform that allows the creation of custom chatbots for Facebook Messenger. Chatfuel uses natural language processing to analyze user requests and provide appropriate responses.

Tars: Tars is a cloud-based chatbot platform that allows the creation of custom chatbots for Facebook Messenger, WhatsApp, and other messaging channels. Tars uses natural language processing to analyze user requests and provide appropriate responses.

MobileMonkey: MobileMonkey is a cloud-based chatbot platform that allows the creation of custom chatbots for Facebook Messenger, Instagram, and SMS. MobileMonkey uses natural language processing to analyze user requests and provide appropriate responses.

Botsify: Botsify is a cloud-based chatbot platform that allows the creation of custom chatbots for Facebook Messenger, WhatsApp, and other messaging channels. Botsify uses natural language processing to analyze user requests and provide appropriate responses.

In summary, there are several pre-packaged solutions available to integrate Chat GPT with social media, allowing businesses to create custom chatbots and advanced virtual assistants that can interact with their customers on social media platforms. These solutions include ManyChat, Chatfuel, Tars, MobileMonkey, and Botsify, offering advanced features to create custom chatbots and virtual assistants on various social media platforms.

Pre-packaged chatbot solutions offer a wide range of advanced features, including:

Natural Language Processing: All major pre-packaged chatbot solutions use Natural Language Processing (NLP) to analyze user requests and provide appropriate responses.

Intent Analysis: Intent analysis helps understand the purpose behind a user's message and provide a suitable response. This feature enables chatbots to deliver more accurate and relevant answers.

Text Generation: Text generation allows chatbots to automatically generate responses without relying on predefined answers, making conversations more fluid and natural.

Third-Party Integrations: Pre-packaged chatbot solutions can integrate with third-party platforms like CRM, marketing automation software, customer support systems, and more.

Conversation Analysis: Conversation analysis helps examine chatbot conversations to identify common user issues, improve chatbot responses, and optimize interactions.

Multilingual Support: Pre-packaged chatbot solutions often provide multilingual support, enabling chatbots to communicate with users in different languages.

Personalization: Pre-packaged chatbot solutions often include personalization features, such as creating customized responses based on user information like name, age, and preferences.

It is possible to customize your chatbot to respond based on your users' preferences. There are several pre-built chatbot solutions that offer personalization features, allowing chatbots to collect user information and use it to provide personalized and relevant responses.

For example, chatbots can collect user information such as name, age, gender, geographic location, and personal preferences, and utilize this information to deliver personalized responses. Additionally, chatbots can use conversation analysis to identify common user issues and tailor responses to meet specific user needs.

Pre-built chatbot solutions often offer customization features that allow chatbot owners to create personalized responses based on user information. For instance, some chatbot solutions enable owners to create responses customized to the user's geographic location or product preferences.

Moreover, by integrating third-party tools with pre-built chatbot solutions, you can gather user information from various sources, such as social media, customer support systems, or CRM software, and use this data to personalize chatbot responses.

In summary, you can personalize your chatbot's responses based on user preferences using pre-built chatbot solutions that offer personalization features. These functionalities enable chatbots to collect user information and utilize it to provide personalized and relevant responses.

Personalizing your chatbot for user preferences offers several advantages, including:

Improved User Experience: Personalizing your chatbot allows you to provide enhanced user experiences by offering relevant and customized responses to user inquiries.

Increased Efficiency: Personalizing your chatbot helps automate user requests, leading to improved customer service efficiency and reduced wait times for users.

Higher Conversion Rates: Personalized responses can increase the likelihood of converting users into actual customers by offering tailored solutions to their needs.

Error Reduction: Personalized responses result in more accurate and pertinent information, reducing the chance of errors and enhancing service quality.

Cost Reduction: By automating user requests, personalization helps lower customer service costs and improves overall business productivity.

However, there are situations where personalizing the chatbot may not be necessary or suitable. For instance, if user requests are very generic and do not require specific user information, a standard response provided by the chatbot may be sufficient.

Privacy of Users: If the nature of information requested by the chatbot concerns the privacy of users, it may be necessary to limit chatbot personalization. For instance, if the chatbot requires personal user information such as phone numbers or home addresses, it may be necessary to restrict the use of this data to avoid privacy issues.

Lack of User Information: If there is insufficient information about users to personalize the chatbot, it may be challenging to provide relevant and personalized responses. In such cases, using standard responses or offering human assistance might be more effective.

Complex Technical Requests: If user requests involve technical or specialized knowledge, chatbot personalization alone may not be sufficient to provide accurate responses. In such cases, involving a human expert might be necessary to provide assistance.

The customization of the chatbot is beneficial in various scenarios, including:

Customer Service: Chatbot personalization is particularly useful for customer service. Chatbots can be customized to provide appropriate and relevant responses to user inquiries, reducing wait times, and improving the overall user experience.

Sales Automation: Chatbot personalization is useful for sales automation. Chatbots can be personalized to collect user information and offer personalized product recommendations, increasing the chances of converting users into actual customers.

Technical Support: Chatbot personalization is valuable for technical support. Chatbots can be personalized to provide specific responses to user requests regarding technical issues, reducing wait times, and enhancing the overall user experience.

Training: Chatbot personalization is useful for training. Chatbots can be personalized to provide specific and relevant information to users based on their learning needs, improving the overall effectiveness of training.

Marketing: Chatbot personalization is useful for marketing. Chatbots can be personalized to provide information about the company's products and services and engage users in personalized marketing conversations, increasing the chances of converting users into actual customers.

In summary, chatbot personalization is beneficial in a wide range of scenarios, including customer service, sales automation, technical support, training, and marketing. It allows chatbots to provide appropriate and relevant responses, improving the overall user experience and increasing the chances of converting users into actual customers.

You can customize your chatbot to meet the specific needs of your business. There are several pre-built chatbot solutions that offer customization features, allowing chatbot owners to create personalized and relevant responses based on their business's specific requirements.

Personalizing your chatbot may include creating personalized responses based on your business, products or services, geographic location, and branding needs. For example, you can personalize your chatbot responses to include specific information about your product or service, such as features, prices, customization options, or delivery times.

Additionally, you can customize your chatbot responses to be consistent with your brand identity. This can include using your company's colors, logos, and images, as well as adopting the appropriate tone in the chatbot conversation.

Personalizing your chatbot to respond in multiple languages can be a great strategy to reach a global audience. Here are some advantages of customizing your chatbot to respond in multiple languages:

Accessibility: Customizing your chatbot to respond in multiple languages allows you to reach a global audience and provide assistance to users of different languages. This increases your user base and enables you to reach new markets.

Improved User Experience: Providing personalized responses in different languages enhances the overall user experience. Users are more likely to use your service if they can communicate in their preferred language.

Increased Efficiency: Customizing your chatbot to respond in multiple languages automates the handling of user requests in different languages, increasing the efficiency of your customer service and reducing wait times for users.

Competitiveness: Customizing your chatbot to respond in multiple languages makes you more competitive in the global market. This can enhance your reputation and brand value.

Higher Sales Potential: Customizing your chatbot to respond in multiple languages allows you to provide personalized product recommendations based on the user's preferred language. This increases the chances of converting users into actual customers and boosts your sales volume.

The most common way to monetize a language model-based chatbot like GPT-3.5 is by using it for customer support or selling products and services. Here are some detailed steps on how to start a revenue-generating activity with a GPT-based chatbot:

Identify your target audience: The first step in monetizing a GPT-based chatbot is to identify your target audience. What are their needs? What are their problems? What are their interests? Once these factors are identified, you can create a chatbot that provides relevant and personalized responses.

Choose a chatbot platform: There are several chatbot platforms to choose from, some of which offer advanced features for chatbot personalization, such as creating personalized responses based on the user's preferred language. Once you've selected a platform, you can start creating your chatbot.

Customize your chatbot: Personalizing your chatbot is crucial for providing relevant and personalized responses. This may involve creating customized responses based on your business, products or services, geographic location, and branding needs.

Integrate your chatbot with your website or online store: After creating your chatbot, you can integrate it with your website or online store. This allows users to access the chatbot directly from your website or online store, improving the overall user experience.

Use your chatbot for customer support or selling products and services: Your chatbot can be used for providing customer support or selling products and services. This can increase your sales volume and enhance the overall user experience.

Monitor your chatbot's performance and optimize it: Monitoring your chatbot's performance, such as user conversion rate, user requests, and user feedback, allows you to optimize its performance and improve the overall user experience.

There are multiple ways to earn with a GPT-3.5 based chatbot, including:

Developing and selling personalized chatbots: One of the main opportunities to earn with a GPT-3.5 based chatbot is by developing and selling personalized chatbots for businesses and individuals. You can offer your chatbot development and customization services at a fixed price or on an hourly basis.

Offering consulting services: If you have a deep knowledge of chatbots and artificial intelligence, you can provide consulting services to businesses that want to use a GPT-3.5 based chatbot to enhance their operations. You can offer advice on how to create and configure a chatbot, how to integrate it with other technologies, and how to optimize its performance.

Selling pre-packaged chatbots: If you prefer not to develop custom chatbots, you can create and sell pre-packaged chatbots for various industries. For example, you can create a customer support chatbot, an appointment booking chatbot, or a sales chatbot for businesses. You can sell these chatbots at a fixed price or through a subscription model.

Offering training services: If you are experienced in using GPT-3.5 based chatbots, you can provide training services to businesses and individuals who want to learn how to use these tools. You can conduct seminars and workshops to explain the basics of using chatbots and provide practical examples of how to use them to improve business efficiency.

Selling access to conversation databases: If you have developed a GPT-3.5 based chatbot that has interacted with numerous users, you can sell access to the conversation database to third parties. This can be useful for businesses that want to analyze user conversations to gain insights into customer needs and desires.

Offering data analysis services: If you have data analysis skills, you can offer data analysis services to clients using GPT-3.5 based chatbots. You can use data analysis tools to extract valuable information from chatbot conversations and provide detailed reports on chatbot usage patterns and user behaviors.

Selling monitoring and maintenance services: If you have developed a GPT-3.5 based chatbot for a client, you can offer monitoring and maintenance services to ensure that the chatbot functions correctly and stays up-to-date. You can monitor the chatbot's performance, troubleshoot technical issues, and update the chatbot with new features.

Offering integration services: If you have experience in software development, you can offer integration services to clients using GPT-3.5 based chatbots. You can integrate the chatbot with other business applications, such as CRM, ERP, and marketing automation software, to optimize business efficiency.

Selling access to plugins and applications: If you have developed plugins and applications for GPT-3.5 based chatbots, you can sell access to these tools to clients. For example, you can create a plugin to integrate the chatbot with Facebook Messenger or an application for creating surveys with the chatbot.

Offering marketing services: If you are skilled in digital marketing, you can offer marketing services to clients using GPT-3.5 based chatbots. You can use the chatbot to create automated marketing campaigns, send personalized messages to users, and improve customer retention.

It's important to note that earning online with GPT Chat requires time, effort, and specific skills. However, here are some steps to get started:

Acquire expertise in chatbots and artificial intelligence: To earn with GPT Chat, you need to acquire specific skills in chatbots and artificial intelligence. You can take free or paid online courses, attend workshops, or read books and articles on the topic.

Identify market opportunities: Once you have the skills, it's essential to identify market opportunities. For example, you can assess the demand for custom chatbots in a specific industry or identify user needs to develop a chatbot that addresses their requirements.

Choose the right platform: There are various platforms for chatbot development, such as Dialogflow, IBM Watson, Microsoft Bot Framework, Amazon Lex, and many others. It's crucial to choose the platform based on project needs and your technical skills.

Developing custom chatbots: Once you have identified a market opportunity and chosen the right platform, you can develop custom chatbots for businesses or individuals. You can offer your development and customization services at a fixed price or on an hourly basis.

Offering training and consulting services: If you are experienced in using chatbots, you can provide training and consulting services to businesses and individuals who want to learn how to use these tools. You can conduct seminars and workshops to explain the basics of using chatbots and provide practical examples of how to use them to improve business efficiency.

Selling access to conversation databases: If you have developed a chatbot that has interacted with numerous users, you can sell access to the conversation database to third parties. This can be useful for businesses that want to analyze user conversations to gain insights into customer needs and desires.

Offering data analysis services: If you have data analysis skills, you can offer data analysis services to clients using chatbots. You can use data analysis tools to extract valuable information from chatbot conversations and provide detailed reports on chatbot usage patterns and user behaviors.

Selling access to plugins and applications: If you have developed plugins and applications for chatbots, you can sell access to these tools to clients. For example, you can create a plugin to integrate the chatbot with Facebook Messenger or an application for creating surveys with the chatbot.

Offering marketing services: If you are skilled in digital marketing, you can offer marketing services to clients using chatbots. You can use the chatbot to create automated marketing campaigns, send personalized messages to users, and improve customer retention.

Monetizing data collected by chatbots is a delicate activity and depends on privacy and personal data protection regulations in your country. Before considering any form of data monetization, it's important to ensure you have obtained user consent for the collection, processing, and use of personal data.

That being said, here are some options for monetizing the data collected by chatbots:

Selling aggregated data: If you have collected a large amount of data, you can sell aggregated data to third parties, such as market research or advertising companies. Aggregated data does not include personally identifiable information but rather anonymous and aggregated statistics.

Offering personalized services: Using the data collected by the chatbot, you can offer personalized services to users, such as product or service recommendations based on their interests and behaviors. These services can be offered for a fee or as part of a broader service package.

Creating machine learning models: Using the data collected by the chatbot, you can create machine learning models to improve the chatbot's effectiveness. These machine learning models can be sold to third parties who want to use these tools to enhance the effectiveness of their chatbots or other AI-based products.

Offering targeted advertising: Using the data collected by the chatbot, you can offer targeted advertising to users. This can be done discreetly, using user data to offer relevant and meaningful advertisements, rather than sending intrusive or annoying ads.

Development of Data-Based Products: By using the data collected from the chatbot, you can develop new products or services based on the needs and desires of users. For instance, you can create a new product based on the information gathered from chatbot conversations, thereby creating a new market or fulfilling an existing need.

Privacy and data protection regulations vary based on the country and region where you operate. Nevertheless, there are some international laws and regulations you should be aware of if you intend to monetize the data collected from chatbots. Here are some of the main ones:

General Data Protection Regulation (GDPR): GDPR is a regulation of the European Union concerning the privacy of personal data. The regulation requires companies to protect users' personal data and obtain their consent for data collection and usage. If you operate in Europe, it is crucial to comply with GDPR to avoid sanctions and fines.

California Consumer Privacy Act (CCPA): CCPA is a law in California, United States, which mandates that companies respect the privacy of users' personal data. The law requires companies to provide users with information about the categories of personal data they collect, how the data is used, and the option to deny consent for data collection.

Japan's Personal Data Protection Act: Japan's Personal Data Protection Act requires companies to protect users' personal data and obtain their consent for data collection and usage. The law also requires companies to provide users with information about the categories of personal data they collect and how the data is used.

Australia's Privacy Act: Australia's Privacy Act mandates that companies protect users' personal data and obtain their consent for data collection and usage. The law also requires companies to provide users with information about the categories of personal data they collect and how the data is used.

Obtaining user consent for the collection and usage of personal data is an important responsibility for anyone operating with chatbots as it can influence users' trust in your services. Here are some guidelines for obtaining user consent for data collection and usage:

Provide clear and transparent information: Furnish users with clear and transparent information about the categories of personal data you collect, how the data is used, storage methods, and any data sharing with third parties.

Request explicit consent: Ask users to explicitly provide their consent for the collection and usage of personal data. Using checkboxes or acceptance buttons can help ensure users have indeed given their consent.

Offer choices: Provide users with choices regarding the collection and usage of personal data. For instance, offer users the ability to choose which personal data they wish to share and for what purposes.

Review and update consent periodically: Periodically review and update user consent for data collection and usage. Make sure to inform users about any changes to your privacy policies and request their updated consent.

Respect privacy regulations: Comply with the privacy regulations of your country or region concerning data collection and usage. Ensure you are aware of applicable laws and regulations and adhere to them.

In summary, obtaining user consent for data collection and usage requires clarity, transparency, and respect for users' privacy. Provide clear and transparent information, request explicit consent, offer choices, review and update consent periodically, and respect privacy regulations in your country or region.

In Italy, the main legislation regarding privacy and personal data protection is the "Codice in materia di protezione dei dati personali," also known as the "Privacy Code" or "D.lgs. 196/2003." However, starting from May 25, 2018, the Privacy Code has been replaced by the General Data Protection Regulation (GDPR) of the European Union.

The GDPR is a harmonized regulation at the European level and applies to all companies that collect, process, or use personal data of European citizens, regardless of their geographical location. The GDPR has introduced new obligations for companies concerning the protection of personal data and has strengthened the rights of users regarding the collection, processing, and usage of their personal data.

In addition to the GDPR, Italy also has the "Garante per la protezione dei dati personali," an independent authority responsible for ensuring the protection of users' personal data and enforcing privacy regulations. The Garante is responsible for providing guidance on privacy regulations, monitoring companies' compliance with the regulations, and imposing sanctions in case of violations.

The General Data Protection Regulation (GDPR) of the European Union has introduced several rights for users concerning the collection, processing, and usage of their personal data. Here is an overview of the main user rights provided by the GDPR:

Right to Information: Users have the right to be informed clearly and transparently about the methods of data collection, processing, and usage of their personal data.

Right of Access: Users have the right to access their personal data and request information about how it is processed and used.

Right of Rectification: Users have the right to request the correction of their personal data in case of inaccuracies or incompleteness.

Right to Erasure (or "Right to be Forgotten"): Users have the right to request the erasure of their personal data in certain circumstances, such as when the data is no longer necessary for the purposes it was collected.

Right to Restriction of Processing: Users have the right to request the restriction of the processing of their personal data in certain circumstances, such as when they contest the accuracy of the data.

Right to Data Portability: Users have the right to request the transfer of their personal data to another company in a structured and machine-readable format.

Right to Object: Users have the right to object to the processing of their personal data for legitimate reasons, such as direct marketing purposes.

Additionally, the GDPR requires companies to inform users clearly and transparently about their rights regarding personal data protection and to respect those rights. Companies must provide procedures for users to request these rights and respond to users' requests within a limited timeframe.

In summary, the GDPR has introduced several rights for users regarding the collection, processing, and usage of their personal data. Users have the right to be informed clearly about the personal data collected, corrected, and deleted, to restrict the processing of their data, and to obtain their personal data in a structured and transferable format. Companies must respect these rights and provide procedures for users to request them.

The General Data Protection Regulation (GDPR) of the European Union imposes significant sanctions on companies that do not comply with privacy and personal data protection rules. Sanctions can be administrative or criminal and depend on the severity of the violation. Here is an overview of the sanctions provided by the GDPR:

Administrative Sanctions: Administrative sanctions can be imposed up to a maximum of 4% of the company's annual turnover or up to 20 million euros, depending on which of these amounts is higher. Administrative sanctions can be imposed for violations of privacy and personal data protection rules, such as failure to obtain user consent for the collection and usage of personal data or failure to notify a personal data breach.

Criminal sanctions: Criminal sanctions can be imposed in cases of severe violations of privacy and personal data protection rules. The penalties can include up to a maximum of 2 years of imprisonment for company executives or data processors.

Additionally, the GDPR allows users to seek compensation for damages suffered as a result of a violation of privacy and personal data protection rules. Companies that fail to comply with the GDPR may be subject to damage claims from users.

To avoid sanctions resulting from the violation of the General Data Protection Regulation (GDPR) of the European Union, companies can take several actions. Here are some of the key actions that companies can take:

Adopt a clear and transparent privacy policy: Companies should adopt a clear and transparent privacy policy that provides detailed information about the methods of data collection, processing, and usage of users' personal data. The privacy policy should be easily accessible and understandable.

Obtain explicit consent from users: Companies should obtain explicit consent from users for the collection, processing, and usage of their personal data. The consent should be obtained clearly and transparently and should be documented.

Implement adequate security measures: Companies should implement adequate security measures to protect users' personal data. These measures may include access controls, encryption, regular backups, and constant system monitoring.

Appoint a Data Protection Officer: Companies should appoint a Data Protection Officer (DPO) who is responsible for the protection of users' personal data and compliance with privacy regulations. The DPO should be an expert in privacy and personal data protection.

Train the staff: Companies should provide regular training to the staff on privacy regulations and personal data protection. The staff should be aware of privacy rules and the company's responsibilities concerning the protection of personal data.

Respect users' rights: Companies should respect users' rights regarding the collection, processing, and usage of their personal data. Users should be informed of their rights, and user requests should be handled promptly and professionally.

As for the suggestions on how to earn money online, there are indeed many possibilities. Some of them include:

Working as a freelancer: You can offer your services online as a freelancer in various fields, such as writing, programming, design, marketing, or translation. Online platforms like Upwork, Freelancer, or Fiverr can help you find freelance work.

Creating a blog or YouTube channel: You can create a blog or a YouTube channel on a topic of your interest and monetize it through advertising, sponsorships, or selling related products/services.

Participating in online surveys: Some companies offer the opportunity to participate in online surveys and earn money or points that can be converted into cash.

Selling products online: You can sell products online on platforms like Amazon, eBay, or Etsy.

Investing in cryptocurrencies: You can invest in cryptocurrencies like Bitcoin, Ethereum, or Litecoin, but it's essential to remember that investments always carry some level of risk.

Working as a freelancer is a very popular option to earn money online. Essentially, freelancers are professionals who offer their services independently, without being tied to a company or an employer. Freelancers can work in various fields, such as writing, programming, design, marketing, or translation.

Here are the main steps to become a freelancer:

Identify your area of expertise: The first step to becoming a freelancer is to identify your area of expertise. Consider what field you have specific skills and knowledge in and where you feel most comfortable. For example, if you are good at writing, you can offer your services as a copywriter or content writer.

Create an online portfolio: Building an online portfolio is essential for showcasing your skills and previous work to potential clients. It's a collection of your best work, and it helps clients understand your capabilities.

Join freelance platforms: There are many freelance platforms available where you can create a profile and start bidding on projects. Some popular platforms include Upwork, Freelancer, Fiverr, and Guru.

Market yourself: As a freelancer, marketing yourself is crucial to attract clients. Use social media, networking, and online communities to promote your services and build a strong reputation.

Set competitive rates: Determine competitive rates for your services, considering factors like your experience, skills, and market demand. Be open to negotiation with clients while maintaining a fair compensation for your work.

Deliver high-quality work: Providing high-quality work is essential to build a good reputation and secure repeat business and positive reviews from clients.

Maintain professionalism: Always communicate professionally with clients, meet deadlines, and be responsive to inquiries. Professionalism is key to establishing long-term relationships with clients.

Becoming a successful freelancer takes time and effort, but with dedication and perseverance, you can establish a rewarding online freelancing career.

Creating an online profile: Once you have identified your area of expertise, you need to create an online profile on a freelance platform like Upwork, Freelancer, or Fiverr. Your profile should include an accurate description of your skills, experiences, and qualifications, along with examples of your previous work.

Finding jobs: After creating your profile, you can search for jobs that match your skills. Freelance platforms offer a wide range of jobs in various industries, from short-term projects to long-term contracts.

Setting the price and rate: Once you have found a job, you need to define the price and rate for your work. You can choose to charge a fixed price for the job or an hourly rate. The price should be fair and competitive compared to other freelancers in the field.

Work hard: Once you have secured a job, work hard to complete it within the agreed-upon timeframe and with the highest possible quality. Your reputation as a freelancer depends on the quality of work you provide.

In summary, working as a freelancer is a popular option for earning money online. To become a freelancer, you need to identify your area of expertise, create an online profile, find jobs, set the price and rate, and work hard to deliver professional and high-quality work.

Here are some of the most popular freelance platforms:

Upwork: Upwork is one of the largest freelance platforms worldwide, with over 12 million registered freelancers and 5 million active clients. Upwork offers jobs in various sectors, including writing, programming, design, marketing, and translation.

Freelancer: Freelancer is another highly popular freelance platform with over 50 million registered users worldwide. Freelancer offers jobs in various sectors, including writing, programming, design, marketing, and translation.

Fiverr: Fiverr is a freelance platform specializing in short-term jobs, with a base price of $5 per job. Fiverr offers jobs in various sectors, including writing, programming, design, and marketing.

Guru: Guru is a freelance platform offering jobs in various sectors, including writing, programming, design, marketing, and translation. Guru has over 3 million registered members worldwide.

PeoplePerHour: PeoplePerHour is a UK-based freelance platform offering jobs in various sectors, including writing, programming, design, and marketing. PeoplePerHour was founded in 2007 and has over 2.5 million registered members worldwide.

Toptal: Toptal is a freelance platform specializing in programming, design, and development jobs. Toptal selects only the best professionals in the industry, offering clients the top talents available.

Here's a brief guide on how to register on some of the major freelance platforms:

Upwork:

To register on Upwork, you need to visit the Upwork website and click on the "Sign Up" button. Then, you need to enter your name, email address, and create a password. Afterward, you'll need to complete your profile and provide details about your work experience and skills. Once your profile is complete, you can start searching for jobs and sending proposals to clients.

Freelancer:

To register on Freelancer, you need to visit the Freelancer website and click on the "Join" button. Then, you need to enter your name, email address, and create a password. Afterward, you'll need to complete your profile and provide details about your work experience and skills. Once your profile is complete, you can start searching for jobs and sending proposals to clients.

Fiverr:

To register on Fiverr, you need to visit the Fiverr website and click on the "Join" button. Then, you need to enter your name, email address, and create a password. Afterward, you'll need to complete your profile and provide details about your work experience and skills. Once your profile is complete, you can create your "gigs" (services you offer) and start looking for clients.

Guru:

To register on Guru, you need to visit the Guru website and click on the "Sign Up" button. Then, you need to enter your name, email address, and create a password. Afterward, you'll need to complete your profile and provide details about your work experience and skills. Once your profile is complete, you can start looking for jobs and sending proposals to clients.

PeoplePerHour:

To register on PeoplePerHour, you need to visit the PeoplePerHour website and click on the "Join" button. Then, you need to enter your name, email address, and create a password. Afterward, you'll need to complete your profile and provide details about your work experience and skills. Once your profile is complete, you can start looking for jobs and sending proposals to clients.

Toptal:

To register on Toptal, you need to visit the Toptal website and click on the "Join Toptal as a Freelancer" button. Then, you need to enter your name, email address, and create a password. Afterward, you'll need to complete your profile and provide details about your work experience and skills. Once your profile is complete, Toptal will evaluate your application and, if selected, connect you with clients.

There are many other freelance platforms you may consider. Here are some other options:

99designs: 99designs is a platform specialized in graphic design, offering jobs such as logo design, website design, packaging design, and more.

SimplyHired: SimplyHired is a global job search platform that allows freelancers to find jobs in various sectors, including writing, programming, design, and marketing.

Topcoder: Topcoder is a platform specialized in software development and design, offering jobs such as app development, website design, and more.

Bark: Bark is a freelance platform that allows freelancers to find jobs in various sectors, including writing, programming, design, and marketing.

TaskRabbit: TaskRabbit is a freelance platform specialized in home maintenance jobs, such as cleaning, gardening, and repairs.

Hirable: Hirable is a freelance platform offering jobs in various sectors, including writing, programming, design, marketing, as well as legal, medical, and financial fields.

Workana: Workana is a freelance platform offering jobs in various sectors, including writing, programming, design, and marketing, with a strong presence in Latin America.

Here are some freelance platforms that offer jobs in specific sectors:

TranslatorsCafe: TranslatorsCafe is a platform specialized in translation, offering translation jobs in various sectors, including legal, medical, technical, and commercial.

ProZ: ProZ is another platform specialized in translation, providing translation jobs in different sectors, such as legal, medical, technical, and commercial.

Shutterstock: Shutterstock is a platform specialized in photography and video, enabling photographers and videomakers to sell their images and videos to clients worldwide.

Getty Images: Getty Images is another platform specialized in photography and video, allowing photographers and videomakers to sell their images and videos to clients worldwide.

Voices.com: Voices.com is a platform specialized in voice-over and dubbing, allowing voice actors and artists to find jobs in various sectors, including advertising, film, animation, and gaming.

ArtStation: ArtStation is a platform specialized in digital art, enabling digital artists to sell their artwork and find jobs as concept artists, character designers, and illustrators.

Musicbed: Musicbed is a platform specialized in music for video production, allowing musicians to sell their music and find jobs as composers and music producers.

Please note that each platform has its own policies, requirements, and registration procedures, so it is essential to carefully read the instructions and provide accurate and truthful information to maximize your chances of finding work.

Many freelance platforms offer opportunities even if you don't have professional experience. However, most clients prefer to hire freelancers with at least some experience in the industry they are looking for workers. If you lack professional experience, you could consider seeking jobs that require basic skills or start with low-cost projects to gain experience and build your portfolio. Some platforms, like Fiverr, also offer low-cost jobs, such as simple writing or graphic design projects, which can be a good starting point for beginners.

Additionally, you might consider participating in free or low-cost online courses to acquire new skills and improve your knowledge. There are numerous online resources available for skill improvement, such as video tutorials, online courses, and free tutorials.

In general, it's crucial to be transparent about your experience and skills when seeking freelance work and provide an accurate and truthful portfolio to showcase your abilities. Over time and with experience, you can increase your reputation and visibility on freelance platforms, accessing more lucrative jobs.

Creating a blog or a YouTube channel can be an option to earn money online. Here are some steps you can follow to create a blog or a YouTube channel:

Choose the topic of your blog or YouTube channel. It's essential to pick a topic you are passionate about and can attract an audience.

Create your blog or YouTube channel. You can use platforms like WordPress for creating a blog or YouTube for a channel.

Produce high-quality content. Whether you're writing blog posts or creating YouTube videos, it's important to generate informative, helpful, and engaging content for your audience.

Promote your blog or YouTube channel. You can promote your blog or channel through social media, online forums, and other marketing channels.

Monetize your blog or YouTube channel. You can monetize your blog or channel through advertising, sponsorships, or selling related products/services.

Continue creating high-quality content and engaging with your audience to increase visibility and popularity.

Remember that creating a blog or a YouTube channel takes time and commitment, but it can be a rewarding source of passive income once you've built a loyal audience.

There are various ways to promote your blog or YouTube channel and increase visibility and audience engagement. Here are some suggestions:

Utilize social media: Promote your content on social media platforms such as Facebook, Twitter, Instagram, LinkedIn, and others. Share your blog posts or videos and use relevant hashtags to reach a broader audience.

Create a newsletter: Establish a newsletter for your readers or viewers to keep them informed about new content and updates.

Collaborate with other bloggers or YouTubers: Look for other bloggers or YouTubers who cover similar topics and collaborate with them to create joint content or promote each other.

Use SEO: Ensure that your blog or YouTube channel is optimized for search engines by using relevant keywords, meta descriptions, and compelling titles.

Engage in online communities: Participate in online communities such as discussion forums, Facebook groups, or relevant subreddits to promote your content.

Offer free content: Provide free content such as guides, ebooks, or useful resources to your audience and promote them through social media or other marketing channels.

Participating in events and conferences: Attend relevant events and conferences related to your topic and promote your blog or YouTube channel through networking and direct promotion. Remember that promoting your blog or YouTube channel requires constant time and commitment, but it can help you reach a broader audience and build your reputation as a blogger or YouTuber.

Here are some tips to optimize your blog or YouTube channel for search engines:

Use relevant keywords: Incorporate relevant keywords in the title of your blog or video, as well as in the description and tags. Utilize tools like Google Keyword Planner or Ubersuggest to find relevant keywords for your topic.

Create high-quality content: Generate informative, helpful, and engaging content for your audience. Search engines reward high-quality content with better rankings in search results.

Use appropriate meta descriptions and tags: Include appropriate meta descriptions and tags for your posts or videos. Meta descriptions and tags provide valuable information to search engines about the content of your blog or YouTube channel.

Create a clear and simple URL: Craft a clear and simple URL for your blog or YouTube channel. A straightforward URL helps search engines identify your blog or channel more effectively.

Use high-quality images and videos: Incorporate high-quality images and videos in your posts or videos. High-quality visuals enhance the user experience and can improve rankings in search results.

Promote your blog or YouTube channel on other websites: Promote your blog or YouTube channel on other websites relevant to your topic. This can help enhance the authority of your website or YouTube channel in the eyes of search engines.

Optimize site or channel loading speed: Ensure that your website or YouTube channel loads quickly. Websites or channels with slow loading times may be penalized by search engines.

Utilize a responsive design: Use a responsive design for your website or YouTube channel. A responsive design allows your website or channel to adapt to different screen sizes, improving the user experience and search result rankings.

Use internal and external links: Incorporate internal and external links in your posts or videos. Internal links enhance website or channel navigation, while external links can increase the authority of your website or YouTube channel in the eyes of search engines.

Create a sitemap: Generate a sitemap for your website or YouTube channel and submit it to search engines. A sitemap provides a list of all the pages on your website or channel, helping search engines identify your content more effectively.

Utilize social media: Promote your blog or YouTube channel using social media. Social media can help generate traffic to your website or

YouTube channel, improving search result rankings.

Create evergreen content: Produce evergreen content, which remains relevant over time. Evergreen content can attract consistent traffic to your website or YouTube channel over time.

Utilize structured data: Use structured data to provide detailed information about your content to search engines. Structured data can improve your positioning in search results and help generate more qualified clicks.

Beware of search engine penalties: Be cautious of search engine penalties such as duplicate content, artificial link building, low-quality content, or spam techniques. Such penalties can harm the ranking of your website or YouTube channel in search results.

After creating your profile on a freelance platform, you can access the "search for jobs" or "find jobs" section. In this section, you will have the opportunity to search for jobs that match your skills.

Freelance platforms offer a wide range of jobs in various sectors, including:

Writing and translation: Jobs in this sector include writing articles, creating web content, translating texts, proofreading, writing resumes, crafting speeches, and much more.

Design and development: Jobs in this sector include creating websites, web programming, graphic design, logo creation, image editing, and much more.

Marketing and advertising: Jobs in this sector include managing advertising campaigns, creating content for social media, social media management, writing marketing emails, creating advertisements, and much more.

Administration and support: Jobs in this sector include email management, calendar management, file management, database management, technical support, and much more.

Professional services: Jobs in this sector include consulting, accounting, human resources management, project management, and much more.

Once you find jobs that match your skills, you can apply for the job by providing a detailed proposal that explains how you intend to handle the work and your rates. Remember that competition can be high for some jobs, so it's essential to submit a high-quality proposal that showcases your experience and skills.

Here are some additional details about searching for jobs on freelance platforms:

Filter search results: Most freelance platforms allow you to filter search results based on category, job type, budget, and other criteria. Use these filters to find the most relevant jobs for your skills.

Read job descriptions carefully: Before applying for a job, read the job description carefully and make sure you fully understand the client's needs. This way, you can submit a high-quality proposal that meets the client's requirements.

Check client reviews: Many freelance platforms allow clients to leave reviews about freelancers. Check client reviews to get an idea of their experience working with the professional. This will help you assess if the client is reliable and if it's worth applying for the job.

Submit a high-quality proposal: When applying for a job, present a high-quality proposal that showcases your experience and skills. Provide detailed information about your approach to the work, your rates, and your expertise in the subject matter.

Maintain communication with the client: Once you've secured the job, it's essential to maintain regular communication with the client to ensure you meet their needs. Respond promptly to their questions and provide regular updates on the status of the work.

Maintain a good reputation: To succeed as a freelancer, it is essential to maintain a good reputation. Complete the work promptly and with high quality, meet deadlines, and communicate clearly with clients. This will help you obtain positive reviews and secure future jobs.

Here are some tips for building a strong freelance portfolio:

Choose your best works: Select your top-quality works for your portfolio. Choose projects that demonstrate your skills and expertise clearly and convincingly.

Showcase your variety: Ensure you include a variety of works in your portfolio to demonstrate your versatility. Also, include projects that showcase your ability to adapt to different styles and client needs.

Describe your projects: Provide detailed descriptions of your projects in the portfolio. Explain your role in the project, the challenges you faced, and how you resolved any issues. This demonstrates your competence and project management abilities.

Use visual media: Utilize visual media such as images, videos, and graphics to showcase your projects effectively. Include screenshots of your work, presentation or demo videos, and other visual elements to make your work stand out.

Highlight the results: Demonstrate the results you achieved with your projects. For example, if you created a successful advertising campaign, include the results like increased sales or website traffic.

Regularly update your portfolio: Keep your portfolio up-to-date with your latest works. This way, potential clients can see that you are active and continuously working on new projects.

Seek feedback from clients: Request feedback from your clients on your projects and use this feedback to continuously improve your work. Including positive feedback in your projects will show your ability to meet clients' needs.

A well-crafted and up-to-date portfolio can help demonstrate your experience and skills as a freelancer, ultimately assisting you in securing future jobs.

Also, personalize your portfolio for specific jobs: If you are seeking work in a particular industry or for a specific type of client, customize your portfolio to cater to their needs. For example, if you are looking for graphic design work for a fashion company, include projects that showcase your expertise in fashion design.

Ask for others' opinions: Seek feedback from friends, colleagues, or industry professionals on your portfolio. Ask for honest feedback and use it to improve your portfolio.

Be selective: Choose the works you include in your portfolio carefully. Select those that best represent your skills and demonstrate your problem-solving ability and ability to meet client needs.

Add an "About Me" section: Create an "About Me" section in your portfolio to introduce yourself to potential clients. Include a brief biography, your skills, and work experience. This helps clients get to know you and your abilities better.

Include a "Testimonials" section: Include a "Testimonials" section in your portfolio where your clients can leave feedback and reviews of your work. This can help demonstrate your experience and your ability to meet clients' needs.

Showcase your creativity: Display your creativity and ability to think outside the box in your portfolio. Include projects that showcase your ability to find creative solutions to clients' problems.

Use keywords: Use keywords in your portfolio to help potential clients easily find your work. Use relevant keywords related to your industry and skills.

Pay attention to design: Pay attention to the design of your portfolio. Ensure that the design is professional, attractive, and easy to navigate. Use high-quality images and a clean and organized layout.

Include personal projects: Include personal projects in your portfolio to demonstrate your creativity and passion for your work. This also shows your ability to work independently and find innovative solutions to problems.

Be authentic: Be authentic and honest in your portfolio. Do not exaggerate your skills or accomplishments. Always be transparent with potential clients and demonstrate your ability to work ethically and professionally.

Include successful projects: Include successful projects in your portfolio. These projects should demonstrate your ability to solve problems and meet clients' needs effectively.

Show your education: If you have specific education or certifications, include them in your portfolio. This can help demonstrate your expertise in your field and increase your credibility as a professional.

Show your evolution: Showcase your evolution as a professional in your portfolio. Include your early works and your most recent projects to demonstrate your growth and ability to continuously improve.

Pay attention to presentation: Pay attention to the presentation of your portfolio. Ensure that it is easy to navigate, and projects are organized logically. Use high-quality images and detailed descriptions to showcase your work.

Include a "Work Process" section: Include a "Work Process" section in your portfolio, explaining your approach to work and the process you follow to complete projects. This demonstrates your professionalism and ability to manage projects effectively.

Show your personality: Display your personality in your portfolio. Include elements that show your creativity, sense of humor, or passion for your work. This can help potential clients connect with you on a personal level.

Be specific: Be specific in your portfolio. Describe exactly what your skills are and how you have solved your clients' problems. This demonstrates your ability to work with focus and meet clients' needs.

Pay attention to details: Pay attention to every detail of your portfolio. Ensure that images are well-cropped and that descriptions are written clearly and correctly. Pay attention to graphic details, such as color and font choice, to highlight your work.

Include diverse projects: Include diverse projects in your portfolio to demonstrate your versatility. For example, if you are a graphic designer, you could include branding projects, web design, and packaging design.

Pay attention to typography: Be mindful of your choice of fonts in your portfolio. Use legible and professional fonts to ensure that project descriptions are easy to read.

Use clear language: Use clear and simple language in your portfolio. Avoid technical jargon and explain your projects in a way that anyone can understand.

Include volunteer projects: If you have volunteered or worked on pro bono projects, include them in your portfolio. This demonstrates your passion for your work and your ability to use your skills to help others.

Include a "Contact" section: Include a "Contact" section in your portfolio where potential clients can find your email address, phone number, and social media profiles. This makes it easier for potential clients to contact you to discuss potential work.

Share your portfolio on social media: Share your portfolio on your social media profiles like LinkedIn, Twitter, or Instagram. This can help promote your work and reach a wider audience.

Include ongoing projects: If you are currently working on a project, include it in your portfolio. This demonstrates your ability to handle complex projects and your attention to detail.

Be consistent: Maintain consistency in the presentation of your portfolio. Use the same graphic style for all your projects and ensure that your portfolio has a cohesive and professional look.

Include an "Accolades" section: If you have received awards or recognition for your work, include them in your portfolio. This demonstrates your expertise and ability to produce high-quality work.

Be open to criticism: Be open to criticism and feedback on your portfolio. Use the feedback to improve your work and better meet your clients' needs.

Include projects that demonstrate your teamwork skills: If you have worked on projects where you collaborated with other professionals or a team, include them in your portfolio. This demonstrates your ability to work collaboratively and handle complex projects.

Include projects that demonstrate your industry knowledge: Include projects that demonstrate your knowledge of your industry. For example, if you are a copywriter, you could include content marketing or newsletter creation projects.

Pay attention to the consistency of tone: Be mindful of maintaining a consistent tone in your portfolio. Use the same writing style for all project descriptions and ensure that the tone is professional and coherent.

Include projects that demonstrate problem-solving skills: Include projects that demonstrate your problem-solving skills. Describe the problem the client had and how you found an effective solution.

Include projects that demonstrate your adaptability: Include projects that demonstrate your ability to adapt to client needs. Describe how you changed your approach to meet the client's requirements.

Use the right amount of information: Use the appropriate amount of information in your portfolio. Avoid including too many technical details or overly long descriptions. Be concise and include only the most important information.

Include projects that demonstrate your time management skills: Include projects that demonstrate your time management skills. Describe how you planned and managed the project effectively.

Include projects that demonstrate your communication skills: Include projects that demonstrate your effective communication skills. Describe how you communicated with the client during the project and how you handled any communication challenges.

Pay attention to client privacy: Be mindful of client privacy in your portfolio. Do not disclose confidential information about clients or their projects without their permission.

Stay up-to-date: Stay updated on the latest trends and technologies in your industry. Keep your portfolio up-to-date and include projects that demonstrate your knowledge of the latest industry trends.

Include projects that demonstrate your ability to innovate: Include projects that demonstrate your ability to innovate. Describe how you used new technologies or creative ideas to solve the client's problem.

Include projects that demonstrate your budget management skills: Include projects that demonstrate your ability to manage your client's budget. Describe how you planned and managed the budget effectively.

Include projects that demonstrate your deadline management skills: Include projects that demonstrate your ability to manage deadlines. Describe how you planned and managed the project to meet the deadlines.

Use interactive presentation: Use an interactive presentation for your portfolio. For example, you could create a website or an interactive PDF document that includes videos, animations, or other interactive features.

Include projects that demonstrate your ability to achieve results: Include projects that demonstrate your ability to achieve results for the client. Describe how your work helped the client achieve their business goals.

Pay attention to the quality of images: Pay attention to the quality of images in your portfolio. Use high-quality images that effectively showcase your work.

Include projects that demonstrate your content creation skills: If you are a copywriter or a content creator, include projects that demonstrate your content creation skills. For example, you could include blog writing projects, video creation, or podcast production.

Include projects that demonstrate your brand creation skills: If you are a graphic designer, include projects that demonstrate your ability to create brands. Describe how you created an effective brand that accurately represents the client.

Include projects that demonstrate your ability to improve results: Include projects that demonstrate your ability to improve the client's results. Describe how you made improvements to the client's previous work and how this led to better results.

Be original: Be original in your portfolio. Use a unique and creative design to showcase your work and attract the attention of potential clients.

Participate in online surveys: Some companies offer the opportunity to participate in online surveys and earn money or points that can be converted into cash. These surveys are used by companies to gather information about their products or services, their reputation, and their competitors. Survey participants are selected based on their demographics and preferences, so it is important to provide accurate information during registration. Participating in online surveys does not require any particular skills and can be an easy and quick way to earn some extra money.

Sell products online: You can sell products online on platforms like Amazon, eBay, or Etsy. You can sell handmade products, vintage products, or new products that you have purchased and want to resell. It is important to choose the right products and set competitive prices to attract customers. Additionally, you will need to manage product shipments and returns, so being organized and reliable is important.

Invest in cryptocurrencies: Cryptocurrencies are digital currencies that use encryption to ensure the security and privacy of transactions. You can invest in cryptocurrencies like Bitcoin, Ethereum, or Litecoin by purchasing them on a cryptocurrency exchange platform. It is important to remember that investments always come with some risk, so thorough research is important before investing, and consulting a financial expert if necessary. Additionally, cryptocurrencies are subject to significant price fluctuations, so it is important to manage the risk and not invest more than you can afford to lose.

To sell products online, you can use platforms like Amazon, eBay, or Etsy, which allow you to reach a wide audience of potential buyers. Additionally, you can create your own ecommerce website to sell your products independently.

The first thing to do is to choose the type of product you want to sell. You can sell handmade products, vintage items, or new products that you have purchased and want to resell. It's important to choose products that are of interest to your target audience and address a specific market need. Additionally, you will need to conduct market research to understand what products are already available on the market and how you can differentiate yourself.

Once you have chosen the products, it's essential to set competitive prices to attract customers. You will also need to manage product shipping and returns, so being organized and reliable is crucial. You can use a shipping service such as USPS, FedEx, or UPS to handle the shipping and delivery of your products.

To promote your products online, you can utilize online advertising, social media, and digital marketing. For example, you can use advertising on platforms like Facebook or Google to reach new customers, or use email marketing to keep existing customers informed about your products and promotions.

In general, selling products online can be an effective way to earn money, but it requires time and effort to manage shipping, returns, and marketing of your products. However, if you are organized and have a quality product, you can create a successful e-commerce business.

Once you have decided on the type of product you want to sell, it's essential to create a detailed and attractive product description. The description should include the features and benefits of the product, dimensions, materials used, and usage instructions. Additionally, you should include high-quality images of the product from different angles, so customers can see the product in detail.

Furthermore, setting competitive prices for your products is essential. You should research the prices of similar products in the market to determine a fair and competitive price. Also, you should consider production costs, warehouse management, shipping, and marketing costs to determine the final price of the product.

For managing shipments, you can use a shipping service like USPS, FedEx, or UPS. You can also use a warehouse management service like Amazon's Fulfillment by Amazon (FBA), which allows you to store your products in Amazon's warehouses and manage shipping and returns automatically.

To promote your products online, you can use digital marketing. For instance, you can use advertising on platforms like Facebook or Google to reach new customers, or you can use email marketing to keep existing customers informed about your products and promotions.

Lastly, providing high-quality customer service is essential. You should respond promptly to customer inquiries and handle returns professionally. This way, customers will be more likely to return for more purchases and recommend your products to friends and family.

Once you have chosen the type of product you want to sell, it's crucial to select the right e-commerce platform for your business. You can use platforms like Shopify, WooCommerce, or Magento to create your online store. These platforms allow you to customize your online store, manage product shipments and returns, handle inventory, and utilize digital marketing tools to promote your products.

To promote your products online, you can use digital marketing. For example, you can use advertising on platforms like Facebook or Google to reach new customers, or you can use email marketing to keep existing customers informed about your products and promotions. Additionally, you can utilize social media to promote your products and engage with your customers.

It's also essential to handle customer reviews professionally. You should encourage customers to leave reviews for your products, both positive and negative. This way, you can use reviews to improve your products and customer service. Positive reviews can also be used as a marketing tool to attract new customers.

Customer service is a crucial aspect of selling products online. You should respond promptly to customer inquiries and handle returns professionally. This way, customers will be more likely to return for more purchases and recommend your products to friends and family.

Lastly, you should continuously monitor sales metrics and website traffic analytics to understand how you can improve your e-commerce business. For instance, you can use analytics tools like Google Analytics to monitor website traffic, conversions, and sales metrics.

To manage the shipping of your products, you can use a shipping service like USPS, FedEx, or UPS. Additionally, you can use a warehouse management service like Fulfillment by Amazon (FBA) from Amazon, which allows you to store your products in Amazon's warehouses and manage shipping and returns automatically. This way, you won't have to worry about shipping management and can focus on promoting your products.

To promote your products online, you can use digital marketing. For example, you can use advertising on platforms like Facebook or Google to reach new customers, or you can use email marketing to keep existing customers informed about your products and promotions. Additionally, you can utilize social media to promote your products and interact with your customers.

It's also important to provide a high-quality shopping experience for your customers. You should ensure that your website is easy to navigate, and products are presented clearly and attractively. Additionally, you should provide detailed product information, such as dimensions, materials used, and usage instructions.

To handle customer service, you should be available to respond to customer inquiries and handle returns professionally. This way, customers will be more likely to return for more purchases and recommend your products to friends and family.

Mailchimp is an email marketing platform that allows you to create and send emails to a broad audience. It offers a range of features, including creating newsletters, personalizing emails, marketing automation, and managing contact lists. Besides email marketing features, Mailchimp also allows you to create landing pages to promote your products or services.

With Mailchimp, you can create personalized emails using pre-designed templates and intuitive design tools. You can also use marketing automation to send emails based on your contacts' actions, such as email opens or cart abandonment. Additionally, you can manage contact lists and segment your audience for targeted email campaigns.

Mailchimp also provides detailed analytics on the performance of your emails, such as open rates, click-through rates, and conversions. This way, you can better understand the effectiveness of your email marketing campaigns and make any necessary adjustments.

Mailchimp offers different pricing plans based on your needs. It also offers a free version that allows you to send up to 10,000 emails per month to a maximum of 2,000 contacts. However, if you want advanced features like marketing automation, you will need to upgrade to a paid plan.

In general, Mailchimp is an excellent choice for small and medium-sized businesses looking to harness the power of email marketing to promote their products or services. It offers a wide range of features and flexible pricing plans, making it suitable for various needs and budgets.

You can use Mailchimp to send emails in different languages. Mailchimp allows you to create customized emails in different languages using pre-designed templates or by creating custom emails from scratch. Additionally, you can use segmentation features to send targeted emails based on your contacts' preferred language.

To create emails in different languages, you can use Mailchimp's multilingual text block. This tool allows you to create a single text block that can be translated into multiple languages. When you send your email, Mailchimp will send the text in your contact's preferred language based on their browser settings or Mailchimp account.

Furthermore, Mailchimp enables you to use the language of your choice when creating your custom email templates. You can also utilize Mailchimp's built-in translator to translate the text of your email into different languages.

In general, Mailchimp is a flexible tool that allows you to create customized emails in different languages, enabling you to reach an international audience and enhance the effectiveness of your email marketing campaigns.

However, Mailchimp does not offer native support for translating images and videos. Nonetheless, there are ways to translate images and videos for your email marketing campaigns on Mailchimp.

For images, you can use online translation tools to translate the text within the image into the desired language. For instance, you can use Google Translate or other online translation tools to translate the text in an image. Then, you'll need to replace the original text with the translated text in the image.

For videos, you can use subtitles to add the translation of the spoken text. You can use online translation tools to translate the spoken text into another language and then add subtitles in the desired language to your video.

In general, translating images and videos requires some manual work, but it can be an effective way to reach an international audience and improve the effectiveness of your email marketing campaigns on Mailchimp.

There are several online translation tools available. Here are some online translation tools that you might find helpful:

Google Translate: Google Translate is one of the most popular online translation services worldwide. It offers translation for text, documents, web pages, and even real-time speech translation.

DeepL: DeepL is another online translation tool that uses advanced artificial intelligence algorithms to provide high-quality translations. It also offers a context-based translation feature that considers the context of the sentence for more accurate translations.

Systran: Systran is another online translation tool that provides translation for text, documents, and web pages in over 140 languages. It also offers specialized translation functions for specific industries like legal, medical, and technology.

These online translation tools can be valuable resources for translating content into different languages for your email marketing campaigns or other projects.

SDL FreeTranslation: SDL FreeTranslation is a free online translation tool that offers text and web page translation in various languages. It also provides advanced features such as document translation and translation with special characters.

Generally, it is not advisable to use online translation tools for translating official documents. Automatic translation tools may be helpful for generic texts, but they cannot guarantee the precision and accuracy required for official documents.

For translating official documents, it is recommended to rely on a professional translator or a translation agency. Professional translators can ensure the accuracy and precision of translations, using the techniques and expertise necessary for official document translation.

Moreover, for some official documents, you may be required to swear before a notary public or a public official that the translation is accurate and correct. In such cases, it is essential to have the translation done by a certified translator who can provide an official translation.

In general, when it comes to official documents, it is important to rely on a professional to ensure the accuracy and precision of the translation. Online translation tools may be useful for generic texts, but they are not suitable for translating official documents.

There are several reliable sources of information on cryptocurrencies. Here are some sources that you might find helpful:

CoinDesk: CoinDesk is one of the leading sources of news and information on cryptocurrencies. It provides news, analysis, market research, and practical guides on cryptocurrencies.

Cointelegraph: Cointelegraph is another source of news and information on cryptocurrencies. It offers news, analysis, guides, and market research on cryptocurrencies.

CryptoSlate: CryptoSlate is a platform for cryptocurrency research and information. It provides news, analysis, market research, and tools for technical analysis of cryptocurrencies.

CryptoCompare: CryptoCompare is a platform for cryptocurrency analysis and comparison. It offers news, market research, technical analysis, and tools for comparing cryptocurrencies.

CoinMarketCap: CoinMarketCap is a platform for cryptocurrency information that provides real-time data on prices, market capitalizations, and other metrics of cryptocurrencies.

Here are some other sources of information on cryptocurrencies that you might find useful:

Bitcoin Magazine: Bitcoin Magazine is one of the earliest cryptocurrency publications. It offers news, analysis, market research, and opinions on cryptocurrencies.

The Block: The Block is another source of news and information about cryptocurrencies. It offers news, analysis, market research, and practical guides on cryptocurrencies.

Decrypt: Decrypt is a website providing news and information about cryptocurrencies, with a focus on privacy and security. It offers news, analysis, market research, and practical guides on cryptocurrencies.

Messari: Messari is a platform for cryptocurrency research and analysis. It offers news, market research, technical analysis, in-depth reports, and tools for cryptocurrency analysis.

Coin Telegraph Markets Pro: Coin Telegraph Markets Pro is a platform for cryptocurrency market analysis and research. It provides real-time data, technical analysis, and tools for cryptocurrency analysis.

The Block: The Block is a platform for news and information about cryptocurrencies and blockchain. It offers news, analysis, market research, and in-depth reports on cryptocurrencies.

Decrypt: Decrypt is a platform for news and information about cryptocurrencies, with a focus on privacy and security. It offers news, analysis, market research, and practical guides on cryptocurrencies.

Messari: Messari is a platform for cryptocurrency research and information. It offers news, analysis, market research, in-depth reports, and tools for cryptocurrency analysis.

Bitcoin Magazine: Bitcoin Magazine is one of the earliest publications about cryptocurrencies, founded in 2012. It offers news, analysis, market research, and practical guides on cryptocurrencies.

Kraken Intelligence: Kraken Intelligence is a platform for research and information about cryptocurrencies managed by the cryptocurrency exchange Kraken. It offers news, analysis, market research, and in-depth reports on cryptocurrencies.

What are cryptocurrencies? Cryptocurrencies are digital currencies that use cryptography to secure and verify transactions and control the creation of new units. Cryptocurrencies are decentralized and are not controlled by a central authority like a central bank.

How do cryptocurrencies work? Cryptocurrencies use a technology called blockchain to record and verify transactions. The blockchain is a public and immutable ledger that securely and transparently records all transactions of a cryptocurrency.

What are the most popular cryptocurrencies? The most popular cryptocurrencies include Bitcoin, Ethereum, Binance Coin, Cardano, Dogecoin, Ripple, and many others. However, the cryptocurrency market is continually evolving, and the most popular cryptocurrencies may change over time.

How can you buy cryptocurrencies? Cryptocurrencies can be purchased through a cryptocurrency exchange platform or through a cryptocurrency broker. Cryptocurrency exchange platforms allow you to buy cryptocurrencies with fiat currency or with other cryptocurrencies.

What are the risks and opportunities of investing in cryptocurrencies? Investing in cryptocurrencies can be risky due to market volatility and the lack of regulation. However, cryptocurrencies can also offer interesting long-term investment opportunities.

What are the current trends in the cryptocurrency market? Currently, the cryptocurrency market is growing, and many cryptocurrencies are reaching new all-time highs. However, the cryptocurrency market is volatile and subject to rapid fluctuations.

What are the differences between cryptocurrencies and traditional currencies? Cryptocurrencies are decentralized and not controlled by a central authority like traditional currencies. Additionally, cryptocurrencies use cryptography to secure and verify transactions, while traditional currencies rely on traditional banking and financial systems.

What are the tax implications of cryptocurrency investments? The tax implications of cryptocurrency investments can vary based on the tax legislation of the country where you reside. In general, cryptocurrency investments are subject to capital gains and losses taxes, but the rules may vary from country to country.

Here are some resources you can use to deepen your knowledge about cryptocurrencies:

Coursera: Coursera offers a wide range of online courses on cryptocurrencies and blockchain. You can take free or paid courses from various universities and institutions, such as Princeton University and the University of California, Berkeley.

Udemy: Udemy offers online courses on various topics, including blockchain and cryptocurrencies. You can choose from free or paid courses.

YouTube: There are many YouTube channels that provide educational videos about cryptocurrencies and blockchain. Some of the most popular channels include Andreas Antonopoulos, Coin Bureau, and Ivan on Tech.

Reddit: Reddit is an online discussion community that includes several sections dedicated to cryptocurrencies, such as r/CryptoCurrency and r/Bitcoin. You can use Reddit to exchange information and opinions with other people interested in cryptocurrencies.

Books: There are many books available on cryptocurrencies and blockchain. Some of the well-known books include "Mastering Bitcoin" by Andreas Antonopoulos, "The Internet of Money" by Andreas Antonopoulos, and "The Basics of Bitcoins and Blockchains" by Antony Lewis.

In conclusion, I hope this introductory book on Chat GPT has provided you with a good overview of this advanced technology and its various applications.

Thank you for taking the time to read this book and for showing interest in learning about new technologies.

Remember that Chat GPT, like any other technology, can be used positively or negatively depending on how it is used. I encourage you to use Chat GPT responsibly and to contribute to its evolution in an ethical and constructive manner. Thank you again for reading this introductory book on Chat GPT!